DODGE VIPER SRT

BY CALVIN CRUZ

BELLWETHER MEDIA • MINNEAPOLIS, MN

D1266690

Are you ready to take it to the extreme?
Torque books thrust you into the action-packed world
of sports, vehicles, mystery, and adventure. These books
may include dirt, smoke, fire, and dangerous stunts.
WARNING: read at your own risk.

This edition first published in 2016 by Bellwether Media, Inc.

No part of this publication may be reproduced in whole or in part without written permission of the publisher.
For information regarding permission, write to Bellwether Media, Inc., Attention: Permissions Department,
5357 Penn Avenue South, Minneapolis, MN 55419.

Library of Congress Cataloging-in-Publication Data

Cruz, Calvin, author.
  Dodge Viper SRT / by Calvin Cruz.
     pages cm -- (Torque. Car crazy)
  Summary: "Engaging images accompany information about the Dodge Viper SRT. The combination
of high-interest subject matter and light text is intended for students in grades 3 through 7"--Provided by
publisher.
  Audience: Ages 7-12.
  Audience: Grades 3-7.
  Includes bibliographical references and index.
  ISBN 978-1-62617-281-4 (hardcover : alk. paper)
  1. Viper automobile--Juvenile literature. I. Title.
  TL215.V544C78 2016
  629.222'2--dc23
                                   2015011007

Printed in the United States of America, North Mankato, MN.

TABLE OF CONTENTS

A NEW VIPER

People gather near the stage at the 2012 New York Auto Show. The crowd waits to see the next **generation** of the Viper **model**. Suddenly, the lights dim and a video plays. Loud music pumps up the room as a light show begins. The crowd cheers as a red Viper rolls in

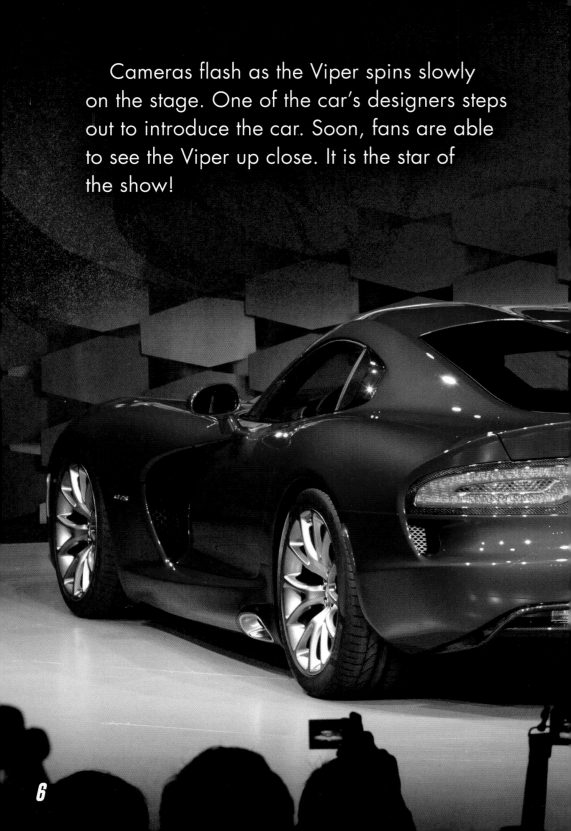

Cameras flash as the Viper spins slowly on the stage. One of the car's designers steps out to introduce the car. Soon, fans are able to see the Viper up close. It is the star of the show!

THE HISTORY OF DODGE

Horace Dodge   **John Dodge**

Growing up, Horace and John Dodge worked on machines with their father. In the late 1800s, the brothers built bicycles. In 1900, the two started their own **machine shop**. They made parts for car companies.

By 1914, the Dodge brothers had begun making their own cars. Their cars were **reliable** and sold at a fair price. The brothers' new company quickly saw success.

SOUTH OF THE BORDER
IN 1916, THE UNITED STATES ARMY USED DODGE CARS IN MEXICO. THEY WERE THE FIRST CARS USED IN COMBAT.

1923 Dodge Brothers Touring

In 1920, the brothers both became ill. Within months, they passed away. The brothers' families sold the company to a bank in 1925. In 1928, Dodge was sold to Walter P. Chrysler.

Walter P. Chrysler

1957 Dodge Custom Royal Lancer

Chrysler made quality cars under the Dodge name. In the 1950s, Dodge began making faster cars that performed well in races. Today, the company makes cars, trucks, and SUVs to meet any driver's needs.

DODGE VIPER SRT

The Dodge Viper was first shown off in 1989 at a Detroit auto show. By 1992, the car was available for purchase. Since then, the Viper's design has changed four times. The newest generation came out in 2013.

Starting with the third generation in 2003, the Viper has been designed by Dodge's SRT team. This stands for "Street and Racing Technology."

1989 Dodge Viper

2013 Dodge Viper SRT

TECHNOLOGY AND GEAR

The Viper SRT's **V10 engine** has ten **cylinders** in the shape of a "V." It starts with the push of a button. The engine is made of **aluminum** to keep it light. It is also made to use as little fuel as possible. It pushes the car to more than 200 miles (322 kilometers) per hour!

V10 engine

Handling is important for a car with such a powerful engine. The Viper's **suspension system** keeps the driver in control in all types of road conditions. The car is short and wide to spread out its weight. Wide tires help the Viper grip the road.

The Viper's body is made to be strong and light. **Magnesium**, aluminum, and **carbon fiber** are used to keep the car's weight down. This helps the Viper be one of the fastest cars on the streets.

SPEED SAVER

ALMOST HALF OF THE VIPER'S BODY IS MADE OF CARBON FIBER. THIS MAKES THE CAR 100 POUNDS (45 KILOGRAMS) LIGHTER THAN IF IT WERE MADE OF METAL.

2015 DODGE VIPER SRT SPECIFICATIONS

CAR STYLE	COUPE
ENGINE	8.4L V10
TOP SPEED	206 MILES (332 KILOMETERS) PER HOUR
0 - 60 TIME	ABOUT 3 SECONDS
HORSEPOWER	645 HP (481 KILOWATTS) @ 6200 RPM
CURB WEIGHT	3,354 POUNDS (1,521 KILOGRAMS)
WIDTH	76.4 INCHES (194 CENTIMETERS)
LENGTH	175.7 INCHES (446 CENTIMETERS)
HEIGHT	49.1 INCHES (125 CENTIMETERS)
WHEEL SIZE	18 INCHES (46 CENTIMETERS) FRONT
	19 INCHES (48 CENTIMETERS) BACK
COST	STARTS AT $84,995

TODAY AND THE FUTURE

The Dodge Viper has been a favorite **supercar** for more than 20 years. Fans love the feel of the car's power and speed. Many Viper SRT owners race their cars. Vipers currently hold records at several racetracks. Vipers will continue to thrill drivers for years to come!

ADDED OPTIONS

DODGE RELEASED TWO SPECIAL EDITIONS OF THE 2015 VIPER SRT. THE VIPER SRT CERAMIC BLUE AND VIPER SRT TA 2.0 OFFER DRIVERS BETTER PERFORMANCE AND COMFORT.

HOW TO SPOT A DODGE VIPER SRT

LARGE CLAMSHELL HOOD

DEEP VENTS

BROAD SHOULDERS

2015 Dodge Viper SRT TA 2.0

GLOSSARY

aluminum—a strong, lightweight metal

carbon fiber—a strong, lightweight material made from woven pieces of carbon

cylinders—chambers in an engine in which fuel is lit

generation—a version of the same model

handling—how a car performs around turns

machine shop—a company that builds or fixes machine parts made of metal or hard plastic

magnesium—a strong, lightweight metal; magnesium is combined with other metals to make lightweight cars.

model—a specific kind of car

reliable—trusted to perform well

supercar—an expensive and high-performing sports car

suspension system—a series of springs and shocks that help a car grip the road

V10 engine—an engine with 10 cylinders arranged in the shape of a "V"

TO LEARN MORE

AT THE LIBRARY

Anderson, Jameson. *Dodge Viper*. Mankato, Minn.: Capstone Press, 2008.

Gifford, Clive. *Car Crazy*. New York, N.Y.: DK Publishing, 2012.

Power, Bob. *Dodge Vipers*. New York, N.Y.: Gareth Stevens Pub., 2012.

ON THE WEB

Learning more about the Dodge Viper SRT is as easy as 1, 2, 3.

1. Go to www.factsurfer.com.

2. Enter "Dodge Viper SRT" into the search box.

3. Click the "Surf" button and you will see a list of related web sites.

With factsurfer.com, finding more information is just a click away.

INDEX

The images in this book are reproduced through the courtesy of: Fiat Chrysler Automobiles/ Flickr, front cover, pp. 12-13, 14, 18, 21 (top left); Chrysler, pp. 4-5, 6-7, 8-9, 10, 12, 15, 16-17, 20-21; epa european pressphoto agency b.v./ Alamy, p. 5 (bottom); Radoslav Nedelchev, p. 9 (bottom); Matthew Richardson/ Alamy, p. 11; Bellwether Media, p. 19.